100 Mandalas Patterns Coloring Book in Black

Thank you for buying my 100 Mandalas patterns book.

This is a great book that will give you the chance to use your creativity, relax and have fun.

Each design is high resolution, printed on its own page in this book 8.5x11 inches and makes every page a creative adventure.

Every image is unique and coloring it will help relieve negative emotions, stress relieving and mental well-being.

You may photocopy the designs for your own use, but please don't share the black and white pages.

Here are a few tips for coloring:

1. Use good quality colored pencils (well sharpened), markers or gel pens.
2. A good choice is also using watercolor pencils, if you are not a beginner.
3. Use a white paper between pages when you color, to protect the next page.
4. Let the background white or color it as you wish. If you want to color it, the best choice is to use soft pastels, but you can also try watercolors, if you're familiar with using them.
5. Color with your favorite music playing in the background, it will help you relax.

Happy coloring!

Jessica Andrews

Colorist's Name
_____

Date
_____

Thank you for buying my 100 Mandalas Coloring book in black, I hope you enjoy it.

This book is the only the third volume of a 3 book series.

Please take a look also at volume 2, "Floral Designs Coloring Book" and Volume 1, "100 Mandalas Coloring Book".

A short review of the book would be very much appreciated!

Yours sincerely,

Jessica Andrews

Copyright © 2017 By Jessica Andrews

This book is © copyrighted by the author, Jessica Andrews and is protected under the US Copyright Act of 1976 and all other applicable international, federal, state and local laws, with ALL rights reserved.

Made in the USA
San Bernardino, CA
05 June 2017